Destination
Success

A Business Fable about School, Work, and Life

Louis Q. Day

ISBN 978-1-64191-276-1 (paperback)
ISBN 978-1-64191-278-5 (digital)

Christian Faith Publishing, Inc.
832 Park Avenue
Meadville, PA 16335
www.christianfaithpublishing.com

Printed in the United States of America

CONTENTS

INTRODUCTION

Why write a book that touches on so many big topics? Let's face it, you could easily write a book on any chapter in this book, as so many of these topics are extremely robust and so important to business and life success. Well, the reason is simple; as a business person and a father of four, these topics have all been so present over the past twelve months with family, friends, and business colleagues, the need became apparent. I have so much passion around the main topics in this book, I wanted to share my thoughts and a few takeaways in each chapter. Everyone who reads this business fable will be drawn to different aspects of the story based on their personal needs or the needs of their family or friends. As I researched the journey from high school to college to the business world, I was amazed at the lack of guidance provided (and accepted) by these young go-getters.

I conducted several mini-experiments when presented with consulting opportunities from young kids and young businesspeople alike. These experiments revealed a couple common themes. First, if someone doesn't have work ethic, drive, and determination to succeed, they will not be successful completing the journey laid out for them. I was really shocked how many people love the thought of self-development but lacked the ambition and focus to make the improvement a reality. The next common thread was how many people are not even aware of the resources that high schools, colleges, and businesses employ to provide developmental opportunities. Recently, I have fielded calls from college students about networking and internships, and during my inquiries, many of them did not realize their colleges had full job-placement departments for the students.

As a young adult, please enjoy the book and always strive for excellence. As a parent reading this book, I would ask you to learn from it but also to take it with a grain of salt. Our children do need to grow up, and we need to give them time and room to do it. When I was twenty-one years old, I did not use my college's job placement center until I graduated (oops). When I was twenty-two years old, I knew I wanted to be a success but had no idea what I wanted to do for a career. This book is designed to get the young people we care so deeply about to avoid making big mistakes that could have a lingering negative impact on their journey. It is also designed to give students and young business people a couple tips that could accelerate their development.

Enjoy the story and go get your dreams.

PREFACE

A Business Fable

My name is JP Clancy, and I like to think I know a thing or two about family and business. After all, I dedicated my adult life to both. I started my business career right after college graduation. I guess you could say that's when I started my business career. It probably did not look that way to the outside world. I begged for a job selling seafood door to door to restaurants for $200/week. Not able to make a living, I also worked evenings stocking shelves at an auto parts store. I am not a handy type of guy at all, but it paid the bills. I didn't care how ground level I was starting because all that mattered to me was getting started fast—why? I met my future wife as a junior in college and knew I needed to close that deal before she wised up and realized she was way out of my league. In addition to closing that deal, I have always been wired to believe I was meant to be some type of a leader of people. Looking back, a NHL hockey coach is still more appealing than what I wound up doing. I can't complain, my journey has been a blast! As tough as those first few months were, I never had doubts about someday "making it." **Mind-set is critical!**

Four relocations and eight major promotions later, I am a director for a Fortune 200 company. Looking back, I can truly say it has been a blur of good fortune, hard work, and a lot of luck! A major takeaway, from my journey, was how hard it was for me to get myself in the right place at the right time. Some may ask, "If it is that hard, is it worth the fight?" My answer would be simple, "Absolutely!" In addition, I would stress the importance of enjoying every step of the journey and to realize every journey looks different. My experience included multiple positions in multiple locations. They included sales, training, marketing, leadership, and managing markets all over the United States.

Looking back, I learned several valuable lessons:

- I now believe I could have been satisfied and successful had I stayed in any of the jobs I rotated through.
- I could live just about anywhere and enjoy it!

I can honestly say prior to living this journey, I would have never thought either lesson mentioned above would have fit into the original plan in my head.

There is one negative about the way I did it; I rushed through every step until I arrived at the corporate headquarters and became a director of training and development. I wish I took more time to enjoy each job and each location along the journey for multiple reasons. First, your long-term runway is built off a combination of your experiences and how you handle each opportunity/challenge along the way. Next, enjoying each stop on the journey is what makes the journey great or not. If you are always distracted by searching for the next opportunity or finding fault with the current one, you will not fully develop or fully assimilate into the life opportunity.

Balancing a career with a growing family is an adventure onto itself. It is so important to communicate and align your goals as heads of the household (sound familiar, businesspeople?). I have always said business relocations are most stressful for those people in the family not starting a new job. They have to make new friends and get acclimated to new schools while the person with the new job is enthralled with the new business adventure. Family alignment and commitment is critical to a successful relocation.

As my kids began to grow up, I coached every sport that would take me (I guess I was always hoping to get discovered by the pro ranks!). I also started volunteering at local high schools, lecturing in the business departments and also got more involved with my local chamber of commerce. It has been fun balancing my current responsibilities at work; trying to give my two high school students a glimpse of the business world and helping companies with less experience solve their challenges. Through all this volunteering, word began to get out about my extracurricular activities and to my astonishment, I have just been asked to give two formal presentations in one day.

The first one is to a group of high school students seeking advice on how to begin to lay a foundation for success during these critical years.

The second presentation is for a group of executives at a local consumer product company. The topic I was asked to speak on at the Consumer Products Company was how to coach their new hires (recent college graduates), as well as their first-line salespeople on career development.

I immediately began to think differently about assembling the content of both presentations. The first question I asked myself was, "Could I use the same presentation for both audiences?" To answer that question, I knew I needed to do some unique pre-work to build these lectures and formulate a plan.

As I began to do my research, I thought, "Who would be the best focus group to derive insights from?" I knew I could look around my headquarter office and ask some suits for their insights, but it seemed so predictable. Then I thought, "Is there an unconventional place to gather valuable insights? Then, it hit me. I walked out of my home office and approached my two oldest daughters (my own high school students). I asked them their thoughts and challenges on what they will have to face after college. They both said at the same time, "That is way too far off to even think about it." I am guessing they hoped I would walk back into my home office, and leave them alone... *Not so fast*. This just reinforced my suspicion; they could be a wealth of information for the presentations. I was getting excited. I did know my main challenge would be I would have to lead the conversation or it wouldn't go anywhere. It would be worth the challenge.

So it was done. My two high school daughters would be my focus group to provide me helpful insights to build a compelling discussion for both groups. *Let the fun begin!*

CHAPTER 1

Only One Chance to Make a First Impression

I started with a dramatic statement to my focus group, Nicole (18), and Marie (16), "You only have one chance to make a first impression! Have you ever made a decision that related to this statement?"

Nicole fired back, "What does that even mean? What decisions are you talking about?"

I responded, "Well, off the top of my head, have you always made great decisions around grades, attitude, work ethic, etc.?"

Nicole said, "Dad, relax, we are going to be fine. You cannot worry about everything."

"Okay," I said. "As long as you are not picky about where you want to go to college."

She defensively replied, "So you don't think I will get into a good school?"

"Well, if you start out slow freshmen year of high school with a 2.8 GPA, do you think you can get it up to a 3.5 GPA by senior year?" I asked.

"I don't know, Dad," she answered.

"Well, if it is not above a 3.5, that will limit your choices of colleges. Now, that being said, Nicole, I am not saying you will not have great schools to pick from, but it will limit you in some way."

Marie said, "So, Dad, we cannot make any mistakes in life?"

Boy, I am either not communicating this well or it is really a challenging topic to grasp.

"Marie, we all make mistakes, and mistakes are a critical part of learning and growing in life." I then added, "You cannot be afraid to make mistakes. A great song by the Goo Goo Dolls says, 'Took it to the edge, now I know why. Never gonna live if you're too scared to die.' I guess the takeaway is, live life to fullest while always trying to do your best for what is right. You know right from wrong. Now go for it!"

"Dad," Nicole shouted, "I feel you are sending mixed messages. First, you say we only have one chance to make a first impression, and next, you tell us everything will work out okay. Which is it?"

"Nicole, I know it can be confusing, but it is really simple: you have to try your best, but you also need to know you will make mistakes. The goal of all this is to minimize the mistakes, and learn from them. Always try to do what's right. Don't forget, you both know the basics: say please and thank you, treat everyone you know the way you want to be treated, dress appropriately. If you're going to an interview, dress professionally. If you're going golfing, wear shorts/skirt and a collared shirt. If you're going to an innovation session, nice jeans and a casual shirt may be perfect. Regardless of the situation, better to air on the side of overdressing versus underdressing. Nicole, if you do the basics while sincerely caring about others, there is a pretty good chance you will do just fine in this world."

After our conversation, I thought of overused phrases I have used in the workplace and at home. One relating to human excellence pops into my mind: "There is nothing worse than wasted potential." It was reinforced in a popular movie from 1993, *A Bronx Tale*, when Sonny says to his young mentee, C, "The saddest thing in life is wasted talent." Imagine being given gifts that we never develop? Gifts that never see the light of day. There are plenty examples all around us. The great city of Boston has been hit with two huge sports-related examples of wasted potential in recent history.

First, the beloved Boston Celtics had the first round pick of the 1986 draft. The Celtics had two picks in that round which was ironic as they were reigning NBA World Champs. With the second pick, the Celtics selected Len Bias from Maryland. Len Bias tragically overdosed on cocaine two days after being selected the #2 overall pick. Talk about wasted talent; he is now remembered as "the greatest player to never play." This is an extreme example of wasted talent due to drug abuse; and it is incredibly sad.

Next is a tragedy of a totally different circumstance. The New England Patriots drafted Aaron Hernandez in the fourth round of the NFL draft. He accomplished something most fourth round picks never dream of: he played so well and showed such incredible potential; he signed a five-year forty-million-dollar contract. People wondered if he would break all-time tight-end records in the NFL. There was only one problem: he ran with the wrong cast of characters and could not break out of a troubled street life. He was accused of hanging around known gang members, and it got worse from there. As a Patriot, he was arrested and indicted for numerous murders, which started in college and included others as a professional athlete. Talk about wasted talent based on hanging with the wrong set of friends and exercising extremely poor judgment that wound up ruining his life, his victims' lives, and his family's life. This story recently ended with another tragic twist as Aaron committed suicide while serving his prison time.

"Girls, I know you must be thinking, Dad, if you are telling us these stories and asking us if you should share them with high school students and young executives, what point are you trying to make with these groups?"

It doesn't matter who you are or where you come from; there are certain fundamental traits found in successful people. They plan to be successful. These incredible people know their purpose, and their why. Every day, they are focused on what they need to do to achieve their purpose. Once they know their purpose, they work at it every day to achieve the vision which is their long-term plan. We will discuss more about purpose later in the book (chapter 4). The two examples above are great reminders. If you work hard at living your purpose, you will actually achieve the greatness, which is your vision. Unfortunately, if you do not live by strong ethical values, your behaviors can lead you down a tragic road of wasted talent. Choices and behaviors matter. Choose wisely!

As we all strive for human excellence, living by virtues is an important step in your development. In each chapter moving forward, I will review a virtue to help make progress and focus on subjects of that chapter.

When you think about making a great first impression, there are many virtues that would be helpful on the journey. Listening, honesty, courtesy, and kindness all are great virtues for making a great first impression. The one that jumps out to me as most important is the virtue of listening while trying to make a great first impression. Why? When you authentically listen to others, you send some strong messages and receive some great benefits:

- You show respect to the person speaking
- You have a greater chance of understanding what they are saying and why they are saying it
- You will be more productive
- You show you care

Merriam-Webster's definition of listen

1. to pay attention to sound
2. to hear something with thoughtful attention
3. to be alert to catch an expected sound

When I meet someone, if they look me in the eyes, ask me about myself, and take a sincere approach to listening to my response, I feel cared about. I feel respected and I want to engage them in conversation. Everyone loves to talk about themselves; it is human nature. It even gets better if someone listens with their complete attention; you can feel it. You feel that they are not listening because they have to, they are listening because they want to.

As a leader in business, sports, family, or anywhere in life, listening is a critical virtue to exemplify. To be a good person and treat others with respect and dignity, listening is a critical virtue to implement. The question is, when others speak to us, do we listen to them or do we just hear them?

> "Most people do not listen with the intent to understand; they listen with the intent to reply." (Stephen R. Covey)

> "The most basic of all human needs is the need to understand and be understood. The best way to understand people is to listen to them." (Ralph Nichols)

These two quotes say a lot. The great business writer and consultant Stephan Covey writes about how people are typically not listening with the purpose of understanding what the other person is speaking about, but instead, they are partially listening while formulating a response. This is so wrong for so many reasons. First, it is disrespectful as the listener is not focusing intently on what the speaker is saying. Next, it is ineffective, because unless you truly hear what is being said and understand why it is being said, you cannot give an authentic, caring, productive response. Listening takes work, energy, concentration, and the discipline not to judge what you are hearing until you hear the whole story and process all the facts.

There was a very famous TV show called *Everybody Loves Raymond* that had a funny episode that centered on active listening. Raymond's young daughter on the show cut off the head of her brother's stuffed animal much to her mom's disappointment. As she was yelling at her daughter for her disappointing behavior, the usually reactionary Raymond took the time to ask his daughter why she did it. During the explanation, his wife interjected, and Raymond asked her to just listen to the whole explanation. After his daughter's explanation and a few clarifying questions, it became obvious their daughter was hurt and disappointed by her parents giving her old stuffed animal to her brother without asking her first. She said she tried to talk to her parents about it, but nobody would listen. Although there was not a legitimate reason to cut up a stuffed animal, they heard her concern and promised never to give her toys away from her without asking first. Before they could yell at her for her unacceptable behavior, she asked if she could have the stuffed animal back to try to fix it for her brother. It was a simple, funny way of reinforcing the importance of completely listening to others and not reacting to half a story or an impression of what happened based on what you imagined occurred.

Everyone wants their story heard. Take the time to listen and hear what others are saying. It is the right thing to do. It will help you make a great first impression.

The other important step everyone should do to make a great first impression is to spend time understanding your personal purpose, values, and vision. Knowing yourself and what you stand for will demonstrate confidence, a strong moral compass, and the ability to focus. Add this to strong listening skills, and you will certainly make a great first impression!

"Most people do not listen with the intent to understand; they listen with the intent to reply."

Stephen R. Covey
(1932-2012)
InspirationBoost.com

Activity for Chapter 1

Instructions:
Finding your why –

Have fun with this exercise as you will revisit some of these topics in future chapters so there will be time to refine your thoughts.

Developing your Purpose - Think through your personal "why". Make notes on what you want to be known for and how you will accomplish it.

What are your values? What behaviors do you want to live by? Will they lead to you achieving your purpose? I always like to list my top 10-20 values and then whittle down the list to 5 values that will be my backbone.

Write your Vision – What is your vision of the future for yourself? Organize your thoughts on where you should be if you are operating on all cylinders in the next 1-3 years.

CHAPTER 2

It Isn't Easy (Getting Started through Preparation and Networking)

We wrapped up topic 1, and I could already see, it is not easy for young men and women to go through high school, start picking colleges, and begin thinking about building careers—talk about overwhelming! But we must forge ahead; that was only the first topic in the talk. Next step: "It Isn't Easy (Getting Started)."

I gathered Nicole and Marie to get started, and before I could introduce topic 2, "It Isn't Easy (Getting Started)," I heard, "Dad, it is not fair to expect me to be able to keep my grades up, have fun, play sports, get excited about picking a college, and then say, 'Everything I do now matters' on top of just growing up."

I had to ask myself, "Was it time to forget about this project and just give my little girl a hug? Was it time to say welcome to the real world, it's not easy and it's not supposed to be easy?"

I was saved by the bell (actually by Marie).

Marie chimed in, "Relax, Nicole! Dad is just asking us questions for a work project. Cut the drama."

Nicole snapped back, "Marie, you're only sixteen, you don't get it."

I jumped in, "Nicole, Marie is right. Remember, I am meeting with you two to learn from you both to see if my views on getting started fast are realistic to share with both high school students and young executives in the same format. I know these questions can be stressful, but can we agree to try to have some fun as you help me?"

They both said, "Okay, Dad."

This was an important moment for me to step in because the pressure Nicole was feeling was real, and pressure on kids today can be a heavy weight. I started to realize, when children are well networked, it can be a blessing and curse. There was no one putting pressure on me when I was seventeen about a successful business career. I knew I had to go to college and graduate; that was it. No pressure on my GPA and certainly none on business expectations. Shockingly, there was not even parental involvement on the major I would pick. It was certainly a different era when compared to the helicopter parents of today. With so much parental involvement, the game is different. When I was a kid, the high school super over-achievers were the only kids that thought of what they wanted to do after college and prepared appropriately. Today, even the C students have their parents making connections for them to get into good schools, work good internships, and come out of college with a good job provided by a family friend. Wow, has the game changed!

With all this anxiety, I wanted to reassure the girls, where there is a will, there is a way. I told them a super-focused, well-networked peer may get a jump start, but talent will win out in the end. The caution here is the talent needs to be observed. The good news is, there are tons of people who enjoy finding and developing talent. I reminded them of my favorite movie, *The Family Man*. Nicholas Cage gets a glimpse into what could have been if his life took a different turn. Both lives were dramatically different, but both lives were wildly successful in their own way. One as a business mogul and one as a family man. During his glimpse of being a family man, NC's character meets the owner of the investment banking company he worked at prior to the glimpse. NC (as the manager of his father-in-law's tire store) famously says to the owner, when he stumbled into the tire store after blowing a tire in his Bentley, "He loves finding talent in obscure places." I have always remembered that scene because in reality, many successful people love to find talent in obscure places (another reason, *everything matters*).

Finding your path is not easy, and it requires a great attitude, persistency, and resiliency. It does *not* require doing everything right from day 1 as demonstrated by two recent encounters I had with graduates from my alma mater. These two individuals both called me looking for their big break in the business world. What struck me was how little they both took advantage of resources offered to them by the job placement center at their college. They were both clueless about how to utilize their network or access other people's network. I asked them if they worked internships their freshman, sophomore, and junior years. They both quickly answered, no. I gave both of them similar advice:

- Synch up with the job placement center at the college to get tips on resume building, interviewing skills, and the network that came there to recruit months earlier.
- I gave them both assignments, relating to relationship building and finding their purpose.
- Lastly, I gave them both the names of individuals to follow up with to network and learn what it takes to succeed.

A funny thing happened here. The two recent graduates took opposite approaches.

The first one was a graduate that did everything right as a student (not necessarily as a career seeker). Her GPA was great. Her volunteer work was exemplary. Her attitude and business appearance were spot on. She read and outlined the book I recommended. She met with my suggested network, and grew her network exponentially by asking my contacts who else they would recommend her meeting. Within weeks, she was well on her way with a couple interviews scheduled. After just months since our first contact, I was thrilled to get an e-mail from her thanking me, and informing me she secured a job with a health care company in Boston—fantastic!

The second graduate talked a great game. College was her playtime. She needed a major transformation just to be ready to sit for an interview. She did not complete any of the homework I assigned her (although was very excited about it when we discussed it). So what did she do? She utilized a family network to get her foot in the door of a company that could provide her valuable experience. It was not completed in the manner I envisioned, but my fingers are crossed she will *learn the game* at this company and start a productive career.

Two totally different approaches, but both produced a favorable outcome. It is hard work getting a shot, and that is just the start; now the real effort is required to show you are worth the investment of the company to develop you. Over twenty-five-plus years in the business world, I have certainly developed opinions on the "right" way to do things, but there are many roads on a successful journey. I have to laugh at myself when I get on a pedestal to talk to my kids about preparing, networking, and the virtue of patience, because I certainly did not have them at the start of my career.

Again, it was time to remind Nicole and Marie what we are doing here. I said, "Girls, don't forget, your dad is preparing to present to two distinctly different audiences and is hoping to use the same presentation for both groups. I want your honest feedback so I can assess if one presentation will hit the mark with both groups. I do not want you two to freak out thinking about your futures. Just so you do not forget, I did not have it all figured out when I was your age, not even close."

As a child, I just believed I would turn out great; there was no strategy, no road map, and certainly no networking involved. I did what I had to in high school to get into a college and did what I had to in college to get a degree, nothing more, nothing less. As far as patience is concerned,… once I started working and realized I will be working for the next forty years, that is where my purpose, vision, and values were born. I was always transparent; I wanted to run a sales group for a Fortune 500 company. The vision was clear. The values and behaviors I set for myself now needed to get me there. I knew in order to get noticed I had to *overperform* at every job. I also knew I needed to have the *best attitude* out of my peers, and I knew

I needed to start letting people *know my goals* (which is networking). As far as the virtue of patience, that is a laugh-out-loud moment! Out of my first six promotions (Dallas, DC, Southern California, and Chicago), it only took months in the position I was just promoted to before I had my eyes on the next job. Why is that bad? First, you need to overperform in every position before you should start thinking about what to do next. Next, it is a little disrespectful to the person that took a shot on you for your current role. They feel as if you are checking the box until a better position opens up. Lastly, you can really enjoy the jobs and locations you are in if you relax and dive all in to the current opportunity and the community you are residing in.

Because I know firsthand how hard it is getting started and waiting for the big break, I go out of my way to help/mentor people on their way up in school or business. Last year was a record year for me as I had twenty people ask me for time to sit with them and give them advice on their career direction. Twenty people! I sat with all twenty people and listened to their goals and dreams. They all have a few common themes:

- I want to get promoted.
- I don't feel like I am a top candidate for promotions.
- Nobody knows my background.

After twenty meetings, my advice was very direct:

- What is your purpose?
- What would you like to be doing in five years?
- How are you perceived in your current job? Does your boss support your development?
- If you worked backward from your five- to ten-year vision, what jobs would help you get that job?
- Who are the people that hire for those jobs? What is your relationship with them? What are you willing to do to move up the relationship pyramid?

I would then ask them to come back with an action plan for improving their relationship with key people. (Include projects that will bring value to them and provide exposure and experience to you), and I would remind them, those projects need to be completed after your regular responsibilities. I would close out every meeting with "This is work, are you up for the challenge?" Twenty for twenty, the answer was yes! I was excited to see who would come back with the best plan.

Nicole and Marie eagerly asked how many people came back with a well-thought-out vision, road map of jobs, list of key people, projects to learn, and built relationships. The answer is one! Yes, one! I am embarrassed for the people that asked for my time, committed to moving their careers forward, and then did nothing. Do you think I would ever consider them for a promotion?

Marie said, "How about the one person that did a well-thought-out plan?"

"That is my friend, Kristen. She has been promoted twice in three years and in line to meet her five-year vision! Preparing, networking, and demonstrating patience works!"

Marie said, "Wow, I want to meet her someday!"

It is important to remember, life is all about self-improvement. That is why I am focusing on a virtue or two in each chapter we can all work on as we seek self-improvement. As stated earlier in the chapter, I want to focus on patience here.

Merriam-Webster's Definition of patience

: the quality of being patient: such as
a: the ability to wait for a long time without becoming annoyed or upset
b: the ability to remain calm and not become annoyed when dealing with problems or with difficult people
c: the ability to give attention to something for a long time without becoming bored or losing interest

Patience is a hard virtue! I actually feel funny writing about patience, as I do not want to imply I have it all figured out. That is certainly not the case! I have studied the virtue as it has long been a personal goal of mine to improve on this virtue. It is hard in our society not to desire instant gratification; it is all around us! I think we all need to slow down and take a deep breath. Remember, St. Augustine said, "Patience is the companion of wisdom." Think of how much better our decisions would be if we stepped back from the situation, evaluated the pros and cons, and made educated decisions. You do not have to look any further than the way we buy cars in the United States. It is the goal of the dealership to sell you the car when you are in their building. The odds of selling you that car if you leave are minuscule. You should go there with a list of the "why" behind your purchase, the pros and cons of the car, the asking price, and the long-term implications of the purchase. But that is not how it works.

Instead of making decisions like that, how much would change if you:

- Stepped back to think
- Evaluated this decision against your short/long-term goals (yes, once again, you need goals)
- Take the emotion out of the decision
- Think or pray about your decision

Then, if you still decide to make the purchase, great! It was a well-thought-out decision that fits into your plan. The example of buying a car is a fun way to look at improving patience. Issues around your reaction to life's unpleasant events can be more challenging. Do you get angry? Do you make rash decisions? Do you get in bad moods when things don't go your way?

Remember, step back to think about whatever the event is and what the best way to react to it is. You may be mad at a professor or at a boss, and in the heat of the moment, you may think it is okay to tell them how you feel. You may feel you do not like them or need them! Is that a true statement or how you feel at that moment? Step back, think of all your goals, take the emotion out of the situation, and then after you think or pray about it, I bet you will make a strong, rational decision. That does not mean you should not have difficult discussions. When you're thoughtful, calm, and organized, those tough discussions go much better!

Build your network!

Activity for Chapter 2

Instructions:

Developing your network –

1. List 5 people that are important to your development (school, business).
2. Assess your relationship with each person. On a scale of 1-4, how do you rate those relationships (1 – they don't know my name, 2 – they know my name but do not know much more than that, 3 – we know each other and I think they like me, 4 – we have a strong relationship and I am confident they would help me achieve a goal)
3. Put together a Plan of Action (POA) to move each person up two levels within a certain amount of time.

CHAPTER 3

Growing Up Nothing Good Happens after 10:00 P.M. (No Matter What Your Age Is)

As I look at my beautiful focus group, the thought of bad decisions in life scares me to death. As a parent, you try to teach your children right from wrong and try to keep them safe. Peer pressure becomes a challenge in high school, crazy temptations become an issue in college, and all those habits become obvious in the workplace. If you develop bad habits as a young adult, it could dramatically affect your success in school or business. So, I began to rack my brain. How do you get through to young people regardless if they are in high school, or just starting a big job after college? Let's face it, we all thought we were invincible at that age.

I am a big fan of real life stories, and I am a huge sports fan. Maybe I could share ... a couple stories of how bad mistakes wrecked promising careers.

Here are a couple of head shaking examples:

Johnny Manziel is an example of wasted talent. Johnny Football, as he became known as a high school superstar, was recruited within his home state of Texas, and attended Texas A&M in 2011 as a redshirt freshman. By the end of his rookie season, he won the coveted Heisman Trophy, and set many school and SEC college records for passing and rushing accomplishments. Johnny Football was on a rocket ship to the top of the football world. He was the number one pick of the Cleveland Browns in 2014. He was the twenty-second overall pick in the NFL draft that year. Talk about living the dream. This Texas A&M superstar signed his big NFL deal reportedly for $8.25 million, including a $4.3 million signing bonus, and about $6.7 million guaranteed. It averages about $2.061 million a year, and included a club option for a fifth year. If you found yourself as the main character in this real life story, all you would have to do is work hard, dedicate yourself to your team and your teammates, and set an example of excellence for all to follow! If you did that, you would earn all the fame and fortune a person could want. So, if I am writing about him in this section of the book, do you think Johnny Football joined the Cleveland Browns, worked hard, dedicated himself to the Browns and to his teammates, and set an example of excellence for all to follow? The simple answer . . .is no! There was an interesting online article in a reputable sports journal called *The Sporting News* published in June of 2016 titled "Johnny Manziel's Antics: 20 Incidents, One Troubled Career." It was sad reading the article that depicted incident after incident that derailed his career. The highlights all seemed to center around excessive alcohol and constant partying, which led to missing meetings and frequently being tardy. There were also claims of drug use, fights, and an abusive environment with his girlfriend (all things that seem to be a common thread with excessive alcohol consumption). Who knows how this story will actually end, but one of the most respected NFL analysts (especially on quarterbacks), ESPN's Jon Gruden, was asked about the chances of Johnny Football returning to the NFL. He said, "I think it's slim right now, but I'm still not going to give up hope," on ESPN's coverage of Monday Night Football in August of 2017. How sad, just three years after the excitement of being drafted and signing a massive deal, this talented individual seems to of let the dream slip away due to irresponsible behavior and a questionable work ethic.

Another recent example is Ryan Lochte. As a family, we watched the 2016 Olympics, and everyone wanted to see if this seven-time medalist could overtake his longtime rival and notably the greatest swimmer ever, Michael Phelps. He had another strong Olympics in which he won several more medals, although he still took a back seat to Michael Phelps. Ryan is not only a world-class athlete, but he had a number of major endorsement deals, which paid him over a million dollars a year. He went public saying he would stay in the game to compete in the 2020 Olympics, which would ensure the spotlight would be kept on him and endorsements would keep coming in. All he had to do was continue down the path he was on. Ryan was in great standing with his team, with USA swimming, and even on the world scene, so he just had to keep the ship steady. The plan changed a little after a party in Rio celebrating the gold medal relay he was on, and he had a little too much to drink. The boys were coming home at 4:00 a.m. (really?)—yes, 4:00 a.m., rather intoxicated and the taxi stopped for a bathroom break at a local gas station. Before you know it, he ripped a sign off the wall (because he was intoxicated and not thinking clearly), and security arrived to arrest the boys.

It went from bad to worse as he generated an international controversy when he falsely claimed that he and three other American swimmers had been pulled over and robbed by armed robbers with police badges while in Rio de Janeiro, Brazil, for the 2016 Summer Olympics. Why did this happen? Did the security forces overreact with guns on the American swimmers? Maybe, but I believe it was the swimmers that caused the problem with poor behavior, and lying about what happened. The two most obvious reasons were the consumption of alcohol and the judgment used to stay out until the wee hours of the night. Ryan's multi-million dollar endorsement deals collapsed over the next week right in front of his eyes.

The girls seemed to understand the Ryan Lochte example. *We are winning.* This is a good sign the girls are getting it. Once again, the whole reason I am doing this project is to connect with high school kids and young executives alike. I crossed my fingers this focus group would help me develop a great presentation for two totally distinct audiences and learn a little something along the way.

I was able to share another example which stayed with me for over twenty-five years. My first big sales meeting, I had the privilege to talk to many senior managers while we sat back and observed the show two district managers put on for the organization. One of the district managers was drinking a Coke and holding court, as he told extremely funny stories about his experiences many years earlier as a brand-new sales rep. The other DM was yelling inappropriate jokes while dancing around; he saw everyone laughing just like they were when the first DM was holding court. The senior leaders pulled me aside and asked if I saw the difference between the two DMs. I was trying to be politically correct and just focused on how funny the first DM was as I did not want to discuss how inappropriate I thought the second DM behaved. Before I could avoid the feedback (or lack thereof) on DM #2, the RM said, "We are laughing *with* DM #1 and laughing *at* DM #2; he will be seriously counseled on his behavior by HR and who knows what the consequence will be."

After reviewing the stories of the two athletes and the business meeting, I felt we needed to close out this discussion with a little chat on why this control is so important. As with the first two chapters, I wanted them to learn about another virtue; this one is called Temperance.

Merriam-Webster's Definition of temperance

1. 1: moderation in action, thought, or feeling: restraint
2. 2a: habitual moderation in the indulgence of the appetites or passions
   2b: moderation in or abstinence from the use of alcoholic beverages

In today's society, this virtue is not too popular. Temperance is concerned with the restraint and moderation of our desires for food, sex, pleasure, and drink. Everything in moderation is okay (at the appropriate stage of one's life: age, marriage, health, etc.). The challenge today is entitlement, ego, pride, and/or a general lack of responsibility for one's actions. This has led to a feeling that everyone has the right to do what they want, when they want, regardless of its effect on one's self or others.

The girls had very valid questions after we discussed temperance.

Nicole said, "Dad, if I go to college next year and announce I am following the virtue of temperance, count me out of going out every Friday and Saturday night. Are you comfortable with me not having any friends?"

I said, "Of course not, Nicole. I am not the fun police. I want you to have the time of your life in college but, I believe you can do that without compromising what you believe in. I know it is hard to stand alone and do the right thing, when so many others are doing the wrong thing and pressuring you. You have to ask yourself, is it worth the risk?"

Marie then asked if those same pressures exist at business meetings. I chuckled, and then said to Marie, "If you do not believe in yourself, everything can be intimidating. As I always tell you, girls, you need to keep your self-esteem high, and stay true to who you are. Marie, remember, I have never had a drink in my business career. I have taken customers to the finest restaurants in the world, played some of the greatest golf courses, hung out at some of the best sports bars, and have never felt pressured into having a drink! Sure, there were plenty of times when less secure people would ask me why I don't drink or tried to talk me into drinking but, I know me and nobody can pressure me into anything. A funny thing has happened at least ten times to me. People I have been at countless business functions with finally noticed I am not drinking and ask if I recently quit. I say, "yes, about thirty years ago!" When you are confident in yourself, you can still be the life of the party. The good news is, you always remember what you said the next day!"

I always tell young executives to keep themselves in control and focused by doing the following:

1. Maintain moderation in everything you do.
2. Be truthful with yourself and identify areas of weakness.
3. Set goals for improvement; write them down to hold yourself accountable.

I always remind them, life is a journey full of ups and downs. Don't get discouraged when you slip up; nobody on this earth is perfect. As I am guiding young adults (or businesspeople), I never call out the virtue of temperance. For some reason, people seem more eager to do something if it is their goal as opposed to an attack on the popular culture of self-absorption and instant gratification.

Behaviors are so important. As students and young executives begin to shape who they are, and what they want to be, it is critical to understand what motivates them, what their goals are, and what is their purpose as they start the journey of life.

The girls asked me, "Dad, what do you mean, what is our purpose?"

I said, "Knowing your life purpose is critical. It keeps you focused and gives you direction in life. Let's talk about knowing your purpose tomorrow."

Activity for Chapter 3

Instructions:

Setting Goals –

1. Think through what is important to you. I mean really reflect on your strengths, weaknesses, dreams, and desires. Make notes on what you hope to achieve.
2. Once you have outlined what is important to you and what you hope to achieve, put these goals on paper. Remember your goals must be specific, make them measurable, make sure they are attainable, and realistic. Lastly, they need to time bound.
3. Once they are down on paper, track your progress. You need to be accountable to yourself.
4. Lastly, don't be afraid to share your goals with loved ones. People close to us can be our biggest supporters.
5. Have fun as you try to achieve your goals. Life is a journey and you need to enjoy the ride.

CHAPTER 4

Find Your Purpose

Well, Nicole and Marie, on to another chapter in this story: "What is a person's purpose? Why is it so important?"

Marie said, "I think your purpose is what you want to do in life."

I replied, "You are certainly on the right track. People look at it in all different ways. I call it your purpose. Some people simply refer to it as what is your why. Some people think of it as their mission."

The girls then asked if I had a "why", I was proud to say yes! They saw the passion in my eyes, and asked me why I was so excited to share it. I wanted to shout, "It is my moral compass in life! It is why I work! It is why I behave the way I do in my personal and professional life! It is reflected in the life lessons I wanted to teach all four of my kids."

My purpose is based on the person I strive to be as well as a combination of all my life experiences. I practically sang my purpose to them:

My purpose is to work every day to maintain the best family possible.

My goal is to teach, protect, and provide for my four kids by role-modeling a strong spiritual lifestyle, while achieving financial success, without sacrificing not being present for the special moments of growing up.

My values are faith, courage, loyalty, love, and listening.

My vision is for each member of our family to become a well-educated, financially secure, contributing member of our community. I wish for all of us to live by a strong value system and build strong, loving families."

Marie said, "Dad, I think it is interesting one of your values is courage. Why courage?"

"Well, that is a great question. I think a successful life takes courage for two main reasons. The first is, it is really hard to live your purpose without messing up. So I think it takes courage to try. The second reason is, if you're open, like I am, people can be very judgmental. They tend to believe a person with a strong purpose is acting 'holier than thou', or is really boring. The truth is, someone who sets a strong purpose knows they will mess up all along the way, but thinks it is worth the challenge to go for it!"

Marie said, "Wow, I cannot believe you put that much thought into your *why*. Was it hard to write?"

I said, "It is a process that takes enormous self-examination, courage, and deep thought."

"A process?" Nicole said. "What do you mean?"

I told her if she followed this simple four-step process, she could begin to create her purpose at this stage of her life:

Process of finding your purpose:

1. List what means the most to you
2. List the values you need to achieve it
3. List why you believe you exist
4. Articulate your purpose in life

Both girls seemed eager to do this exercise as they thought it would be cool to know their why, but Nicole thought she was a little young to do this and said, "How many times am I going to have to do this?"

I couldn't help but laugh and think how different my why would have looked when I was seventeen versus today. I tried to tell her so much is based on the stage of her life, but these guiding principles are so important regardless if you are defining your why as a student, a sibling, a family member, a young businessperson, or thinking through your spiritual "why". The purpose you define can help guide you through all of life's twists and turns.

I told the girls to think about the most soulful singer they have ever heard. Once they had someone in mind, I told them about a video I saw on YouTube. The host of a show was discussing the importance of knowing your why and went on to say, "If someone knows their why, their performance will dramatically improve."

To demonstrate this point, he found a soulful music teacher in the audience and asked him to sing the beautiful song "Amazing Grace." The gentlemen busted out an incredible version of the song. It was just sheer talent! The host then gave him a purpose for singing the song. He told the gentleman to think of someone in life that had incredible challenges. That someone just got out of prison and seems to have made a complete turnaround. They asked for forgiveness and a fresh start. He told the gentleman to think of the joy in seeing this special someone improve their life and celebrate it by singing them this triumphant song. Wow, just thinking of the second version could still knock me off my seat as it was so passionate, soulful—you could feel the joy! It's all about knowing your why.

I think the girls were totally into finding their why and my last example would seal the deal. They love TOMS shoes and they know that when they buy a pair (or when I buy a pair for them), someone in need gets a new pair of shoes from TOMS, as well. What they did not know was the story of the young impressive CEO of TOMS. I was able to explain his background based on a great Harvard Business Review (HBR) article about how the CEO of TOMS shoes (Blake Mycoskie) made an incredible evolution of his own journey through his purpose and the reinvention of himself and his company; talk about gutsy.

After founding TOMS shoes and successfully running the company for six years, Blake shocked the business world by taking a sabbatical. He felt disillusioned even though the company had grown to over 300 million in revenues. He moved back to where he grew up in Austin, Texas, to do some soul-searching. On this journey, he discovered his company began focusing more on process than purpose. His original goal was to use business to improve lives, and boy, did he do it well! He truly believed this purpose gave him a competitive advantage as it helped build an emotional bond with customers and motivate employees. At the end of his sabbatical, he came back to TOMS re-energized, and he was ready to ensure TOMS stayed true to its purpose. He read Simon Sinek's book *Start with Why*. This book reaffirmed the need for having a compelling why. Blake stormed back into the company reinforcing his why by establishing another company, TOMS Roasting, a coffee company. They would donate a week's worth of clean water for every bag of coffee they sold; the energy and passion was back. TOMS just celebrated their tenth year in business and is still following their why of using business to improve lives.

I mentioned the importance of the virtue courage in establishing your purpose and as you saw, it is one of the core values I try to live by.

Merriam-Webster's Definition of Courage

1.   : mental or moral strength to venture, persevere, and withstand danger, fear, or difficulty

Courage is a tough virtue to write about. Is it something you are born with? Is it something you develop? Is it something that occurs instinctually? Well, the purpose of this section is not to debate why some people have courage, some people seem to be overwhelmed with fear and the majority of us seem to be somewhere in the middle.

The purpose of this section is to reinforce the virtue of courage as an important part of life, and we should all seek to improve on it. Courage is truly the opposite of fear and that may be a good place to start. Why do we fear different things? I personally believe it is common to fear the unknown and things we cannot control. I also think many people fear losing something:

-   You don't want to go to the doctor for fear of getting a bad diagnosis.

- You do not stand up for yourself at work because of fear of losing your job.
- You do not defend the kid being bullied because you worry you will be next.

This is where we all need to dig deep and find moral courage. These are issues of right and wrong, and it is everyone's responsibility to find the courage to protect the weak, fight for fairness, and have faith.

As far as heroic courage, which I would say is running into a burning house to save someone, I just hope after a lifetime of choosing right versus wrong and being raised properly, I would find the courage to be heroic.

Exercise for improving your courage:

1. Write down the top five things that you fear.
2. Explore the "what" that scares you about these things.
3. Educate yourself on the what. Read about it; talk to experts.

This summer, I heard a story about a young man who seemingly had it all. He was a great student and a standout athlete in his town. He had nothing but options to pursue to reach his potential. Would it be an academic scholarship? Would it be an athletic scholarship? Would it be a pro sport? He picked the pro sport. He was a young man no one worried about. He always seemed to make the right decisions: keep the grades high, never did drugs, picked the right friends at school while staying focused on pursuing his dream. Now he is with a new crowd and is trying to fit in with a group of professional athletes; he was no longer the guy everybody wanted to be around, he was now the guy that wanted to be accepted. One night after practice, the boys headed out for some partying. Although this was not his scene, he was afraid of saying no. He feared what the other players would say about him if he chose to stay home. So he went; after several drinks, he made up an excuse to leave early, but it was not early enough. On his way home, he was in a terrible car accident and killed a father of two. His life was forever changed as his dreams of being a professional athlete were dashed, and he was off to serve six years in prison for driving while intoxicated during the accident. What a waste of talent! He now travels the country educating high school students on the dangers of drugs and alcohol. He also begs young adults to have the courage to say no and do what's right. He also delivers the message; even if you do not do it, if you permit it, you promote it.

I firmly believe it is the lack of knowledge about something or a situation that causes fear. If you learn more about the topics or get more exposure to them, I find my anxiety is minimized. Courage sometimes comes from experience and knowledge. Go, get it!

Activity for Chapter 4

Instructions:

Establishing your PURPOSE –

In the beginning of this book, you did an exercise on finding your purpose, values and vision. I love that exercise and believe it is critical to moving forward in a strategic manner. I think it all starts with clarity around your purpose so in this exercise, I want you to take a deeper dive into finding and articulating your purpose. Build on what you started in the first activity.

Research and reevaluate your purpose:

1. Educate yourself on leading thought leaders on finding your purpose

    Examples:
    -   Watch Simon Sinek's TED talk on PURPOSE
    -   Read the Harvard Business Review article on Tom's Shoes CEO

2. Find a successful person and interview them on their PURPOSE (their why) and list your major takeaways

3. Revisit your exercise from Chapter 1 . . . . is your PURPOSE the same as you originally wrote? If not, redo it!

CHAPTER 5

Perfecting Your Craft

I think the girls got excited about finding their purpose. Sure, they both thought it was overwhelming, but to actually put time and energy into such a self-fulfilling cause would feel like a labor of love, they thought.

Marie eagerly shouted, "What's next? Once I find out what I am meant to do, am I done?"

That response got Nicole laughing; she gave her the silly look that only a sister could get away with, and then said, "Have you met our dad? Do you really think Dad won't have another assignment after we think through our purpose?"

"Man," I said, "Nicole, that was perfect! Nothing great comes from an idea or even establishing your purpose. Greatness comes from hard work, grit, determination, courage, attitude, and a non-stop commitment to excellence! Another word for all of this pre-work is preparation."

Marie said, "Okay, exactly what do you mean by preparation?"

"Well," I said, "the simple definition is:

Preparation (the free dictionary)

1. The act or process of preparing.
2. The state of having been made ready beforehand; readiness.
3. Often preparations an action done to prepare for something, especially for an event or undertaking.

The kids then gave me the look: Dad, you're beginning to pontificate. I love the process of finding your purpose, but bringing it to life is even more exciting! I started telling the kids when someone is committed to making their dreams come true, and believes they will make it happen, and does all the hard work (more than they even believed they could do), most people start to root for these people's success. If they are athletes trying to make it, do they work out harder than all their peers? Do they get up earlier to workout, stay up later examining their progress/gaps, work on stamina, and work on perfecting their skills? If they are businesspeople, do they study the analytics harder, build relationships deeper, and understand customer insights more? Do they get into the office earlier, is their attitude always positive, and will they stand up for the tough calls? "Girls, my point here is if they do the minimal work that they need to, or even the same amount as all their peers, are they trying to perfect their craft or are they just getting by?"

"Nicole and Marie, we can't forget why we are talking about this. Do you two understand how to be the best? It is hard, right? Well, I need to find a way to teach the high school students and young executives that to be the best, you need to differentiate yourself. They also need to know it is really hard and will require more than just out working the competition. I need to teach them (and you two), it is a journey. So relax, and get ready for the ride. I need your input and perspectives to help me craft the story!"

People who want to be the best do things differently. One of my favorite military leaders has said, "There are no secrets to success. It is the result of preparation, hard work, learning from failure" Colin Powell.

What's different about this Colin Powell quote is where he adds, *learning from failure*. One of history's greatest inventors also said, "Many of life's failures are people who did not realize how close they were to success when they gave up" (Thomas A. Edison).

Failure is OK; it is part of life. Those who embrace it and learn from it often go onto greatness with this newfound knowledge. Look at NFL coaches: if you only gave Bill Belichick one chance (when he coached the Cleveland Browns) for five years, he may have gone down in history as a mediocre at best coach in the NFL (at least for that period). Coach Belichick took those learnings to New England and has won four Super Bowls, six Super Bowl appearances, and will now go down as one of the greatest NFL coaches in history. "Wow," I said to the girls, "What if he shut down after getting fired from Cleveland? What if other NFL teams thought he wasn't worth taking another shot on him? We would not have one of the greatest NFL coaches ever; in addition to being prepared, greatness also requires resiliency and belief."

"So, girls, since we started talking about perfecting your craft, the importance of preparation has been a cornerstone of successful people. Then we talked about Colin Powell saying success is a result of preparation, hard work, and learning from failure. Our quote from Edison then talked about not giving up; it is so important to learn at a young age if you prepare, work hard, and never give up, you have a great chance of finding success in life. It is not easy to perfect your craft, so try your best and enjoy the ride."

I think a virtue that goes well with this topic is humility. I think it is important to start with a few questions: Does our society promote humility? Is it easy to be humble in today's world? Do we have good role models in the business world? Are we addicted to ego?

I was recently reading articles on humility in daily life, and as a business leader, I stumbled across a great article on the Internet by a gentleman named Robert Roberts. Early in his article on humility, he includes a paragraph that really hit home with me: "Benjamin Franklin was very disciplined in his efforts to acquire and maintain the virtues. Looking back on his efforts to gain humility, he comments:

"In reality, there is, perhaps, no one of our natural passions so hard to subdue as pride. Disguise it, struggle with it, beat it down, stifle it, mortify it as much as one pleases, it is still alive, and will every now and then peep out and show itself" (Autobiography).

So why do I include this in a section on humility? Pride is an almost near-perfect antonym for humility. When you put them side by side, here are the definitions of each from Merriam-Webster:

Humility: freedom from pride or arrogance: the quality or state of being humble accepted the honor with humility. The ordeal taught her humility.

Humility, in various interpretations, is widely seen as a virtue in many religious and philosophical traditions, often in contrast to narcissism, hubris and other forms of pride.

Merriam-Webster's Definition of pride

1. the quality or state of being proud: such as: inordinate self-esteem: conceit: a reasonable or justifiable self-respect: delight or elation arising from some act, possession, or relationship parental pride
2. proud or disdainful behavior or treatment: disdain
3. ostentatious display: highest pitch: prime
4. a source of pride: the best in a group or class

Then came the question I wished I did not get.

Nicole said, "Dad, are you humble or prideful?"

I wished I could truthfully fire back that I am a very humble man! That is what I want to be, but if I am to be honest, I had to answer Nicole like this, "I wish I was all humility, but unfortunately, I struggle to get pride and ego out of my life."

Marie immediately asked, "Why?"

"Well," I said, "human nature, our overly competitive world, and our current me, me, me environment make it much easier to let your ego take over than it is to consistently behave in a humble way."

Nicole then said, "Dad, can you give us an example of how you are too egocentric?"

Just what I wanted to do, engage in a discussion about my weaknesses as I put together a talk on how to get life right. I answered her as humbly as possible about my shortcomings. "Okay, Nicole, if we must discuss this, where do I start? Well, I am very concerned about physical appearances, the car I drive, and being seen as a leader at work, all things I wish did not matter to me."

She said, "Wow, Dad, you really need to work on your humility!"

I just had to laugh hard. No matter how successful we become, it is small in such a big world.

Humility is not thinking less of yourself, it's thinking of yourself less.

Activity for Chapter 5

Instructions:

How to live with humility -

1. Pick 5 people you trust that will give you honest feedback and ask them to participate in this self-improvement project for you.

2. Ask those 5 people to really think hard about you over the years and provide you two things that you were too self-confident about, too narcissistic about, or too filled with hubris on… (if they can't come up with two things relating to the downfalls of excessive pride…spin it – have them give you two occasions you could have demonstrated more humility while reacting to the circumstances).

3. Create a wall of improvement – post all 10 ideas on the wall (I recommend putting each one on a different color piece of paper – just for effect). Keep it posted for a couple days and see which 1 you have the most passion to improve.

4. Put together a fun roadmap (plan) for improving it. Be specific, make sure it is possible, set clear time-bound results and track your progress. I would also tell a couple of your mentors to help hold you accountable.

This is a tough activity! Talk about letting your guard down…enjoy it and stay humble!

CHAPTER 6

Accepting Successes and Challenges

"**A**ttitude is everything", I told the girls. I started laughing and said, "Even when you are rewarded with an opportunity, it can take all sorts of turns."

The girls asked what I meant, so I began the crazy story of when I was asked to launch a consumer product for one of my past companies.

I was thrilled! I was handpicked as the head of sales for this launch and it was not just a normal consumer product, but it was supposed to be a Mega-selling product predicted to really help consumers everywhere. What an honor, right? Well in year 1, it was filled with all the excitement. Just imagine preparing for this monumental event. Building the team was the first step. I was allowed to pick my leadership team, and empower them to build their regional and district teams. We had the honor and thrill of branding the team with a name, logo, and a creative multimedia welcome packet. We had an extensive team building meeting and established our team's purpose, values, and vision. Afterwards, we went public and introduced our sales organization to the community. We did it with a lot of swagger and maybe a little hubris (unfortunately). The next year was filled with building relationships and waiting for the big product to hit the market. When the big day finally arrived, we truly felt invincible. All signs were good. Was the market ready for our product? We believed our product would have great differentiation, great presence in retail stores, great consumer appeal, and great consumer benefits. Then, something unexpected happened. One by one, challenges began to overtake the optimism of an ideal selling environment. Selling advantage by selling advantage began to slip away. Product differentiation went from being a perceived advantage to a perceived disadvantaged over the first twelve months. The retail presence of our product went from being a potential competitive advantage to the most challenging retail availability in the company's history. The revolutionary consumer appeal and benefits we planned for appeared to be overpromised, and underdelivered in the minds of our customers. When you add up all those challenges, our destiny was written. We would not be a market leader but instead a smaller product in a huge market. This salesforce never went more than six weeks without a new headwind challenging their ability to sell their product. The sales force could have given up, but instead, they acted like champions and fought on. Because of their attitudes and fighting spirit, the company stood behind them and continued to reward them as appropriately as possible. This prestigious group of salespeople became most proud of being known for their fighting spirit and helping our customers; they truly lived their purpose as an elite sales organization. They always did what was right for our customers even if it meant not recommending our consumer product for certain customers. This impeccable attitude and focus enabled them to accomplish a renowned launch in their business segment and help tens of thousands of consumers—pretty cool stuff!

One of our sales consultants articulated the following quote that resonated with our sales team: "You know as well as I do that often the hand we are dealt is the only one we get to play. We will play the hand we are dealt, be glad to be in the game, and we will play to win no matter the odds. Worry, negativity, blaming others, or a defeated attitude when the game is still on is in no way productive. Great selling results are produced by the perpetual expectation of attaining them. Our fight has just begun."

The team took that quote to heart and, as stated above, accomplished some outstanding results. I said earlier in this chapter, that attitude is everything, and there are no two ways about it; it is a huge factor in dealing with success.

Faith is the virtue that jumps out at me as essential for the long-term ability to deal with success and failure. Faith is an important virtue as you begin your journey into adulthood and as you build your career. Faith is not a guarantee everything will be OK. Faith is the belief that if you give your all, you can battle through anything. Faith and humility will help you deal with successes and keep your challenges in perspective. I reminded Nicole and Marie of a personal event in my life in which faith was a cornerstone in getting through it.

I still remember like it was yesterday. I walked home from school to a friend's house to hang out. We were playing a silly basketball game in his family room when the phone rang. My mom's good friend was on the phone, and she asked my friend John to tell me to come home right away. As I walked up my street, I could see a few cars in my driveway. I actually liked when we had company, so I thought nothing of it. It began to take a different turn as I walked into our family room and saw my mom, sisters, a couple family friends, and our parish priest. I found out that afternoon my father had died suddenly at work. He was walking to lunch with his friends and dropped dead of a massive MI on the street in Philadelphia.

What gets a twelve-year-old boy through such a traumatic event?

Well, there are many things: a loving family, great teachers, caring coaches, and a strong sense of faith. As an adult, I always say, when something like losing your father at twelve occurs, kids can take two different roads. One is a road of "why me." This is a sad road, which becomes a justification for everything that could go wrong in life: nothing is your fault (trouble in school, challenging relationships or excessive partying just to name a few). The other road is largely based on faith. I felt it was important to always believe if I tried my best, somehow everything would work out okay. I also felt this tragedy taught an important lesson on the importance of living every day to the fullest.

Nicole said, "Dad, that is such a sad story." She continued, "I would have not been able to deal with that if something happened to you when I was twelve."

I assured her, "I would have said the same thing when I was a teenager if that had not happened to me. We find strength when we have to, even if we cannot imagine it."

Marie asked, "Do you know other people who went through challenges as tough as the one you went through?"

"Marie," I said, "I know people who have dealt with challenges I cannot imagine dealing with." I went on to tell the girls, "Our world is filled with exceptional people who make sacrifices for others that are mind-blowing. Think about our military, they risk their lives every day to provide us freedom. I had the honor of meeting and listening to a gentleman named Noah Galloway. He is an American hero who was severely injured in the Iraq War. Girls, when I say severely, I mean severely! He lost his right leg and right arm after an explosion and woke up many days later at Walter Reed Hospital in Washington, DC. Upon regaining consciousness, his mother gave him life-changing news about his injuries and personal life which would have destroyed most men. Noah was different though, this was the beginning of rebuilding himself. Since those devastating injuries, he has solidified himself as a hero, great father, role model, competitive athlete (yes, I wrote competitive athlete!), the *Men's Health* Man of the Year, TV star, motivational speaker, and author (book: *Living with No Excuses: The Remarkable Rebirth of an American Soldier*). Noah was a remarkable man to meet. The tragic injuries he endured would have sent most people down the road of *"why me."* Not Noah! He has not only focused on being a great father to his children, but he focused on helping other veterans with their challenges and living every moment of his life to the fullest. Some may look at him and feel sorry for his injuries, but if you truly see the man Noah became post injuries, many may be envious of the man he became. Noah used his faith to overcome his challenges and become an amazing success!

When you truly believe life is a gift, you will enthusiastically try to reach your fullest potential and help others reach their fullest potential.

Accepting successes and challenges in life are many times aligned with the virtue of faith.

The definition from Merriam-Webster's of faith is:

1. a: allegiance to duty or a person: loyalty lost faith in the company's President b (1): fidelity to one's promises (2): sincerity of intentions acted in good faith
2. a (1): belief and trust in and loyalty to God (2): belief in the traditional doctrines of a Religion. b (1): firm belief in something for which there is no proof clinging to the faith that her missing son would one day return (2): complete trust
3. : something that is believed especially with strong conviction; especially: a system of religious beliefs the Protestant faith

As you grow up in high school, college, or as a young businessperson, faith in yourself, faith in your abilities, faith in your employer, and faith in the system (business, life, and religion) is important, but not easy. We live in a cynical society where companies, teachers, people, and religious leaders have let us down. How can we believe? How can we stay focused? Why is it important to have faith? First, there are so many things out of our control. Without faith in what is right and just, everyone would just give up. I have worked with so many talented people who just never landed in the right spot in our company. Some were terminated due to performance, some were terminated due to inadvertently doing the wrong thing without knowing it, and some were terminated because of damaged relationships. They all had a few things in common. They were all talented individuals who truly believed they were unfairly treated by a well-respected company. This is a perfect scenario to lose faith in the system, and blame others for your misfortune. Luckily, these fine people all dug deep to regain their faith in what is right and what they could control. It took all of them different lengths of time to get back to a good spot. I am happy to say, they all landed with companies which turned out to be a better fit for their lifecycle, career goals, and financial needs. Some would say this supports the theory, you should always keep your faith! Everything happens for a reason!

Activity for Chapter 6

Instructions:

Enhancing your faith –

1. Think of situation where something unfortunate has happened to you or a loved one?

2. Look back and analyze that event, can you find any positives that came out of it?

3. Write down everything positive that came out of it and everything you learned from it?

   - Remember, even if you struggled finding a positive, you've learned something... that is a positive. Growth comes from learning!

4. Lastly, put your top positives or learnings on post-it notes and put it somewhere you will see it regularly. It's important to remember faith will get you through life's challenges.

Faith can move mountains and your doubt can create them.

CHAPTER 7

The Importance of Giving Back

"**G**irls, we are in the home stretch, and you have really helped me put together an outline on how I should present the students and young executives a plan on how to succeed. I really cannot thank you both enough. I am starting to see the light. We may really help some talented young folks meet their potential. Now, before we finish, I believe once you teach others to be successful, you also need to teach them the importance of giving back to others."

In order to give back, we all must have clear expectations in our minds of what success is in life, or in others words, what does winning look like.

It was tough to explain to Nicole and Marie that there is great learning from losses as well as wins.

Marie said, "You raised us to win. Won't you be embarrassed if we lose at work?"

I said, "Marie, absolutely not! Just like playing soccer as a twelve-year-old, as long as you bring your very best every day with every challenge, I could never be more proud of you. There will always be opportunities and challenges you need to recognize, strategize on, and execute against."

This was so much for them to comprehend. The idea of learning from losing, and then helping ensure others do not make the same mistake is difficult for a student or young professional.

I asked both Nicole and Marie to answer the question, 'what is winning'. I told them if you asked me when I was twenty-two, I would have said making a ton of money and gaining power (pretty shallow, but I was young). A lot has changed over the years. If I was asked now what business success is at forty-nine, I would say to achieve the business objectives set for my organization while being recognized as a motivational, ethical, authentic leader of people who enhances the lives of those I am lucky enough to have on my team. If it is your goal to enhance the lives of people you work with, you better believe in giving back, mentoring, motivating, developing, and listening to become the center of everything you focus on.

Some great people have various views on what a successful life looks like:

> "At the end of life we will not be judged by how many diplomas we have received, how much money we have made, how many great things we have done. We will be judged by 'I was hungry and you gave me food to eat, I was naked and you clothed me, I was homeless and you took me in.' Hungry not only for bread—but hungry for love. Naked not only for clothing—but naked for human dignity and respect. Homeless not only for want of a room of bricks—but homeless because of rejection." (Mother Teresa)

> "The price of success is hard work, dedication to the job at hand, and the determination that whether we win or lose, we have applied the best of ourselves to the task at hand." (Vince Lombardi)

"The foundation stones for a balanced success are honesty, character, integrity, faith, love and loyalty." (Zig Ziglar)

These three people come from very distinct backgrounds (religion, sports, and business), but their view of success revolves around being the best person they can be, and by doing right by other people. It is very hard in today's society to focus on being the best person you can be, all while thinking about other people's needs. We now live in a "me" society, so everything that is considered cool flies in the face of living a virtuous life. Think of what people get excited about: constantly taking selfies, posting your every move on Facebook, tweeting your every thought, and always doing what you want, when you want. Nicole and Marie started looking at me like I was crazy. Nicole finally said, "Dad, what is so wrong with having fun?"

I said, "Nicole, that is a great point! There is nothing wrong with enjoying yourself and having fun. It is all about balance. I think we have shifted from a hardworking, family-oriented society to a culture of *fun* and *look at me.*"

I love entering a room and seeing pictures of family and friends to activate fond memories. I am not sure when our world went from capturing a precious memory to posting your every move, thinking everyone needs to know what you had for dinner, what cool party you got invited to, or how cool your vacation was.

"Girls, how do we teach our two groups about what to do after you find a little success? They need to know, when you fight the fight, it is your responsibility (no matter what stage of life you are in) to pay it forward. It is so important to give back to others. I think that ties perfectly into the virtue of kindness."

The Merriam-Webster definition of kindness:

1. : the quality or state of being kind *treating people with kindness and respect*
2. : a kind deed: favor *They did me a great kindness.*
3. *archaic*: affection

[1] Aristotle, in Book II of his "Rhetoric," defines it as being "helpfulness towards someone in need, not in return for anything, nor for the advantage of the helper himself, but for that of the person helped."[2]

When I think about being kind or the virtue of kindness, I must be honest; it is hard to always think about helping others when we all have some much going. We are busy, we are tired, we are stressed out, and we have big responsibilities. Where do you find the time and energy to help others?

One of the girls said, "On top of finding the time, when you have so much on your own plate, is it okay to think why should I help others?" She continued, "Isn't it enough to work hard and try to be nice? Do I really have to step over that line and help others?"

I love the honesty of these questions and had to step back and think of the best way to answer her. After a noticeable pause, I said, "Those feelings are 100 percent normal, and there will be plenty of times you just do not have it in you to think and act in service to others. The key is to find balance between yourself and doing good for others." I continued, "I have several mentors who on the surface always find time to counsel and guide me, but is that really the case? When I call my favorite consultant, the former president of my company, or even my uncle, are they just waiting there for my call or text looking to help? Of course not! Even if they receive the call or text on their worst day, they don't just fire back, fix your own problems! I am having a bad day! They are controlled enough, professional enough, and caring enough to pick a time that would work for them and they will call/text me back offering a breakfast or phone call on the day best suited for them. It is all about balance and caring to realize what they are doing matters. It is kind of them because depending on the situation, their mentoring really helps me through challenging life situations. It makes me a better person due to their kindness."

Marie then asked, "Do you mentor other people?"

I think I shocked her when I said, "Yes, formally at work and informally with several college kids."

She asked, "What college kids, and why don't we know about this?"

I reminded her about the statement Aristotle made in the Wikipedia definition of kindness, "Helpfulness towards someone in need, not in return for anything, nor for the advantage of the helper himself, but for that of the person helped—if it is not about me, why would I talk about it?"

Nicole then said, "Why do you help them?"

I replied, "That is simple. When I was graduating college, I did not prepare myself properly through internships. I had no idea what to do the day after graduation. Talk about scary. When a confident person is lost, it is an awful feeling. Then, something pretty cool happened, the harder I worked, the more it appeared people tried to help me, through networks, guidance, and constructive crticism! I wouldn't have been ready for my first big break without them (and their mentoring). Nicole, I will never forget how all those people have helped me throughout my career, and it will always motivate me to try to help anyone that asks. Call it paying it forward, call it learning kindness through others, it doesn't matter what we call it, but it motivates me to do more, to be there for others and to be kind (even when I don't feel like it)."

I reminded the girls, just being nice to people is a form of kindness. I have always been struck by what I believe to be an urban myth about kindness. The story goes like this: A man was driving down the highway and pulled off at a rest area. After using the rest room and getting a refreshment, he was walking by a pay phone (they were necessary before cell phones) and it began to ring. What would motivate someone to pick up a random ringing pay phone? Who knows, but when he did, a timid voice was on the other end of the phone in deep despair. The young woman said she dialed a random number, hoping someone would pick up, so she would tell them her life was meaningless and she was going to end it. As the story goes, the man happened to be a psychologist and talked to the woman for an extended period. The story concludes by saying this connection saved this young woman's life as she felt this stranger listened to her and cared about her (a random call with a random stranger). Is it true? Who knows and who really cares? What is true is you never know what someone else is going through. Therefore, you never know how impactful your random acts of kindness can be. Could you have saved a life just by being nice to someone that is in need?

Activity for Chapter 7

Instructions:

Increasing kindness in this world –

This is a two-part activity:

1.   Look around your current environment (school or work) to see
     if has somebody recently joined your class or business unit? -ask
     yourself:

     - Do they fit in?
     - What can you do to help them fit in and
       feel comfortable?
          * examples:
               - Set up a welcome lunch or even
               buy them a coffee.
                    *When you get together, be prepared to learn about
                    them. A couple examples may be:

                         - What do they do in their free time?
                         - What is their favorite vacation spot?

Remember, when you demonstrate sincere caring, it will mean the
world to others.

2.   Write down three ways you can give back to your community…
     pick one and volunteer. It will help others and you will love the
     feeling of doing good for the sake of just helping others.

Here are a few examples:
     - Visit the elderly at a nursing home
     - Become a mentor (at work or at an
       organization like Big Brothers/Big Sisters)
     - Help at the local food pantry
     - Do a mission trip

CHAPTER 8

The Big Presentation
(Summary)

Holy cow, I thought, my two presentations are today and thanks to my focus group, I actually think I am ready. When I think back over the seven topics I reviewed with these two adorable young women, I believe it is everything I need to teach these two distinct groups. The group of high school students seeking advice on how to begin to lay a foundation for success and a group of executives at a consumer product company on how to get on the path to success.

Now, I am struggling with how I want to tell the story. I am debating if I should start or finish the presentation with a true story. I think this story may help everyone remember some key takeaways of the presentation.

Nicole just sighed as she clearly thought she was done with this project. Thank goodness, Marie asked, "What story are you thinking of Dad?"

I said, "Well, I am glad you asked. My longtime friend, Donny, used to say, 'Always give everything and win life!' I used to always laugh, thinking, it is not even a logistical statement (but never asked for clarification). I thought, "Shouldn't it read," 'Always give everything you have and you will win in life'? Finally, we had the discussion after I had listened to this statement for two years, Don shook his head in disbelief, and said, "No! Stop overthinking everything. It is an acronym for the essential elements of winning in life. Learn it, and live it, my friend!" He then said, "Man, why didn't you ask me two years ago what it meant. I assumed you knew it. Let me spell it out for you. Let's start at the beginning, the A in always means attitude, and I have some firm beliefs around attitude."

<u>A</u>lways <u>G</u>ive <u>E</u>verything <u>A</u>nd <u>W</u>in <u>L</u>ife

A - Attitude

There is a famous statement, "Attitude is everything!" After coaching kids at sports and coaching employees for the past twenty years, if attitude is not everything, it is darn close! One major takeaway for a young person is, like it or not, your attitude tells your story. I love the motivational saying, "A champion gets up even when they can't!" Think about what that means. The weight of the world is against someone, and it is their sheer will and determination that forces them to get up and keep fighting. Their attitude carries them forward. I love movies, and there is a movie franchise called *Rocky*. It is a fictional story (except if you grew up in Philly, most of us would swear we knew him). It's about a street boxer who gets an unexpected shot at the title, but lacks the skills of a great boxer. He has the intangibles: grit, preparation, courage, and commitment that endears him to us. The greatest of his gifts is his attitude. I love it! If you can work on one skill, work on your attitude. Remember, instead of reacting, think about what can you do to make the best of any situation.

G - Grades

It does not matter if I am talking about HS, college, MBA, or your annual performance review at your job. In an ideal world, you rock out good grades from freshmen year on, and ease into the school of your choice. I witnessed a great success story of how it is supposed to work with my good friend's daughter. She did all the right things in high school: good athlete, great character, and super grades. She picked out her school of choice and off went the application. She got admitted into the university but not into the business program she desired. She only had one question for them, "If I ace my freshman year, will you reconsider me for the business program?" When the answer came back yes, she was off to show them she deserved to be in the business program. After a fantastic freshman year, the business school laid out the red carpet for her. If the story ended there, it would be a success, but that is far from the ending. She continued to work extremely hard and, by junior year, had excelled academically and completed several prestigious internships. Hold on, it gets better; by the beginning of senior year, she had an offer from a multinational corporation (which she accepted). Now, that would be a great ending to the story. But hold on one more time! Before Christmas of her senior year, the same company put her name in for a prestigious global assignment. Her competition was the elite of the elite from Ivy League colleges all over the country. You may have guessed it, she got it! Pure work ethic and attitude! That is the ideal route, but it is not for everyone. We all have to be willing to make the effort to excel at school or work, or accept the consequence of that subpar performance. I am not a proponent you need to be in the top 10 percent of your class to get into a good college, or even to get into a good company. I was never the world's best student, and I was always well aware it would make my job search more challenging, and as crazy as it sounds, I was OK with that consequence. My mantra became, "Give me a shot and I will not let you down." I built my story around my attitude and my work ethic, and had to endure plenty of no's before getting my break. That was OK, because I knew it wasn't supposed to be easy, and failure was never an option in my mind. Once I got my big break, there was no looking back! My work ethic and attitude enabled me to get recognized and rewarded. Now my report card (annual performance review) is always in the top 10 percent of the company.

In the smash hit Broadway play *Hamilton*, there is a popular song that states, "I am not throwing away my shot! I am young, scrappy, and hungry, just like my country."

E - Electronic Media

Wow, you talk about a blessing and a curse. Technology is simply unbelievable. If you would have told me I would go from a bag phone (five years into my career) to smart phones, tweets, and instant answers, I would have said you were crazy! As much as I love the instant technology, I worry about all the negatives which go along with it. Once again, whether you're a student or employee, electronic media can hurt as much as it helps.

We recently heard a sad story about high school students. A young girl was infatuated with a young man. As their relationship intensified and hormones raged, the young girl sent an inappropriate image of herself to the love of her young life. Within months, the relationship ended (as the vast majority of HS relations do), and the young couple got hurt feelings and began to throw insults around. This was typical but still very sad. Everyone would wish the story ended there. One of the insults knocked the boy to his knees and he really wanted to win this "fight." Unimaginably, he tried to embarrass the girl and sent the inappropriate picture she had sent privately to him. He sent it to several of their friends, and accomplished his goal. She was mortified! When her parents saw her devastated, they asked why. She told them the whole story, and her father's rage led him right into the principal's office, which led right into the local police department. The nightmare became a reality. A young lady is devastated, and a young man, along with his text friends, all have major life-lasting legal issues.

This story is one of a million examples. Electronic media lasts forever and is there for everyone to see. Remember, we have seen athletes lose millions of dollars due to professional teams seeing stories of drug abuse on electronic media sites. We have also seen college graduates not getting jobs based on an employer screening electronic media sites searching for unbecoming behaviors. Lastly, but certainly not least, if you want a good laugh, ask an IT person at a Fortune 500 company the crazy things they have seen while they wipe a turned-in computer from a terminated employee. Talk about inappropriate (age doesn't seem to help many employees with their judgement)! Don't waste your hard work, behave properly, and be responsible with social media.

A - Appearance

We are living in an era of individualism. It is important to be honest with yourself. Are you looking to fit in somewhere or do your own thing? Unfortunately, the saying "You can't judge a book by its cover", isn't always a reality. People develop perceptions based on many things and one is appearance. We can tell a similar story that we told about grades. Appearance can make your job easier or more difficult, depending on if you want to conform or not. This is not just an old man's view. It is not just saying young adults need to adapt to corporate America and buy winged-tip shoes and navy-blue suits. I recently spent three days at an innovation center and was told to trade in my dress pants and sport coats for jeans, flip-flops, and t-shirts. I adapted, and it was fun! The key is knowing your environment. The old saying "Dress for success" may evolve from looking like the stereotypical business person to adapting to the environment, like I did at the innovation *think tank.*

W - Work Ethic

Your work ethic is obvious for the world to see. You can't fake it. People who have a pure work ethic are so impressive. There is an older gentleman in our corporate offices that cleans the bathrooms in this massive building. All day long, I see Jose walking with a bucket of cleaning agents that looks like it weighs about as much he does. He keeps to himself and keeps our building looking like a palace. I started going out of my way to say thank you and see how he is doing each day. As I got to know him, he is a great man with an incredible family who means the world to him. All you have to do is look at his work ethic to see how much he cares. He works forty hours a week and at a restaurant another twenty hours a week, all to give his family a better life! He is a grateful man for his opportunities and a proud man based on how he is providing for his family.

L - Living Clean

Another tough topic! Many people feel anybody who talks about not drinking or doing drugs (where it is legal) is judging them. I want to start by saying, none of us should judge each other. This is a very serious topic though, and because of the potential consequences that can arise from not living clean, it does need to be discussed. Unfortunately, drugs and alcohol have become common in our society regardless of the devastating effects on families, careers, and society. Here are two startling facts from the National Institute of Alcohol Abuse and Alcoholism: in 2014, 24.7 percent of people ages eighteen or older reported they engaged in binge drinking in the past month and more than 10 percent of US children live with a parent with alcohol problems, according to a 2012 study. I am certainly not judging anyone, but the facts are the facts. The human body is not made to absorb high levels of drugs or alcohol. Heredity can be a factor in developing alcoholism. It is important people understand the risks, although, there are many factors in determining if someone will develop problems with alcohol, and an inherited gene is one of them. My advice is to make good decisions. There are no do-overs in life.

Wow, that last topic was heavy! I laughed while thinking, I wish I knew what *Always Give Everything And Win Life* meant over the past two years; it is really good!

While you are on the journey toward achieving your personal vision, remember to make conscious decisions around attitude, grades, electronic media, appearance, work ethic, and living clean. This should help you realize your potential. Working to fulfill your potential is important for many reasons.

Here is the dilemma, do I use the acronym above, or do I go directly into the presentation?

If I decide not to use the acronym to tell the story, I think I have a strong story flow I can walk the groups through. Let me walk you through it.

How does this sound?

I feel passionate, it all starts with making a great first impression. Regardless of the audience, people must set the stage for success by doing all the small stuff to win the relationship (dress appropriately, tell a great story, and truly listen to what the people around you are saying).

I plan to transition from the importance of making a great first impression to the art of networking and building strong relationships. There are plenty of resources out there including my favorite book on the subject, *The Relation Edge*. I will also stress that growth and development takes time. It is so important to be patient and enjoy the ride. You just may find out the destination you really want is right where you are.

I will then progress from the exciting business skill of networking to a potential career killer. I feel the need to review some basic business behaviors all young students and employees should stay away from; I have never seen excessive drinking and long nights turn out to be a positive! I talked about temperance in chapter 3 and my simple takeaway for these groups will be try to do everything in moderation. I will also emphasize, it can take years to build a great reputation, but it only takes one night to ruin it; be careful!

I will re-energize the presentation by shifting to one of my favorite business challenges: finding your purpose. This is not an easy task as it takes real courage to be honest about what you want to do, then go for it! Once you know your purpose and how you will achieve it (what values you will live by), your work becomes clearer and your motivation is easier to sustain.

Once they understand their purpose (mission) and values, we will talk about outworking everyone else. I will highlight the day-to-day grit required for success. I get excited just thinking about the young people I have worked with that make good life choices, have an extreme work ethic, and are humble. When people have that winning combination, I would put them on any team I was leading. If you want icing on the cake, hopefully, they have overcome failure at some point; that is, when there is real growth.

Next, I will build on this and talk about my favorite topic: attitude. Attitude is everything in my mind. Whether you are competing for college or proving yourself as a young executive, if you have the brains and a great attitude to go along with it, there will be no stopping you! Unfortunately, the other side of that situation is, you could have the brains, you could be a hard worker, but if you have a bad attitude, I would actually work to get you off my team. There is no room for negativity on any of my teams. Sometimes people struggle with attitude, especially when things do not go their way, and I can sympathize with that, up to point. Once it affects team dynamics or productivity, I hit my breaking point. People need to have faith in their abilities, in their team, and their organization that leadership will be honest and transparent about why things work out the way they do.

Last, but not least I will talk to both groups about the importance of giving back and remembering how hard their journey has been. Students and young executives need to understand nothing good comes easy (and it's not supposed to). We live in a period that people believe they deserve a great job and are entitled to success. It requires hard work to acquire the skills necessary to succeed, and if you're lucky, people will help guide you through those lessons. If you are fortunate to have great mentors, pass it onto the next generation of business people. If you were not fortunate to have great mentors, make sure that it doesn't happen to the next generation; be a servant leader. It is all an act of kindness, and simply put, kindness makes the world a better place.

Well, the girls said they liked the flow with or without the acronym story so . . .

It is going to be a last-minute decision, because if I do not leave now, I will be late (and you never get a second chance to make a first impression!). Wish me luck on my presentation! There are a lot of young people getting started, and if they follow the roadmap laid out in this presentation, they will certainly go places. Destination: Success!

My desire for these students and businesspeople is to take this content to heart. Our journey through life will be a better and more fulfilling place if we work on these principles and focus on improving the virtues discussed in this book.

ABOUT THE AUTHOR

Louis Q. Day is an energetic, passionate business leader driven to help others and share his life's learnings. He has succeeded leading large teams for several Fortune 100 companies as well as learned valuable lessons from small- and medium-sized companies.

His proudest accomplishment is his family. Louis has been happily married for over twenty-five years and has four wonderful children. This book arose from his desire to help educate his four kids on some of the valuable lessons he has learned over the years. As he began to mentor young businesspeople and college students, he knew this business fable could help many more people striving for excellence than the original notes he had planned on giving to his children.

Louis always says he has made plenty of mistakes and witnessed countless blunders of people trying to get started in the business world or self-destruct once they got into the business game. So many people asked for a roadmap to success so now he asks you to take the journey to Destination: Success!

CPSIA information can be obtained
at www.ICGtesting.com
Printed in the USA
LVHW071011290719
625697LV00015B/148/P